AIM HIGH

The Heart of God
Volume 1

Kim Holmes

RALEIGH, NORTH CAROLINA

Copyright © 2014 by **Kim Holmes**

All rights reserved. No part of this publication may be reproduced, distributed, or transmitted in any form or by any means, without prior written permission.

Printed in the United States of America 2014—First Edition
Printed in the United States of America 2022—Second Edition

Kim Holmes/Rain Publishing LLC
PO Box 14397
Raleigh, NC 27620
www.rainpublishing.com

Unless otherwise indicated, Scripture quotations are taken from the Authorized King James Version. All rights reserved.

Aim High / Kim Holmes. – 2nd ed.
ISBN 978-1-7346106-6-6

Library of Congress Control Number: 2021922437

Dedication

CHRIST JESUS, I give this book to YOU.
Without YOU Volume 1 of AIM HIGH would have never
made it Into the hands of those who now hold it.
God thank you for being "my HELP." I love YOU.
To my King, my husband, Frank,
A General in God's Kingdom; I salute you!
God truly favored me when He knitted us together for life.
There can never be another,
I will always only have eyes for you.
To my two daughters Ebony & Krystal,
My heritage from the Lord.
We've labored together as a family
and weathered life's toughest storms
You hung in there; this one's for you.
To my growing family, I cannot fail to mention you
The Greatest Gems in all the earth:
My Grandchildren
Isaiah, Arianna, Mayah, Aniyah, and Josiah.
You are the best!
Last, but not least, To my son-in-love, Trevis,
Thank you for assisting me with my cover design.
I love you all and thank our
God daily for graciously gifting me with you.

"For I know the thoughts that I think toward you, saith the Lord, thoughts of peace, and not of evil, to give you an expected end."[1]

CONTENTS

Prayer Brings Answers 1
What Comes to Mind When You Think About The Name, JESUS? 5
A Ripe Harvest 9
Doing Things God's Way 13
At Midnight 17
From   Unforgiveness to Forgiveness... Rx: Until Seventy x Seven 21
No More Excuses 27
NEVER Late... ALWAYS On Time 31
We Must Consider Our Ways 35
WARNING: Your Own Tongue Can Become Your Worst Enemy 39
Leave the Past in the Past 43
What do YOU do When the Issue is YOU? 47
You Owe God Praise 53
Secret Confession 57
Shake The Dust 63
My People shall NEVER be put to SHAME! 67
JESUS is calling YOU 71
ABOUT THE AUTHOR 75
Endnotes 79

For the Hearer

AIM HIGH... is a collaboration of inspired writings spoken from "The Heart of God." Every piece was penned with you in mind. Through each skillfully crafted message, the author seeks to move the hearer beyond mere Christendom as she sets out to conceive and give birth to "the mind of Christ" [2] while waiting in His presence.

She knows because of the issues life brings, that one could easily get stuck within the walls of adversity. However, for the believer, there's hope and assurance that victory is just a prayer away. Her intended goal is to dispel the lies of the enemy as she reaches to engrave in the hearts and minds of others that God can, and God will. Her life serves as proof that you don't have to wait to get to heaven to enjoy life. You can share in the joys of heaven right now here in the earth, in every area of life if you live God's way.

Come up higher and experience the joys of knowing God in a greater dimension.

Together let's enter into HIS presence....

CHAPTER ONE

Prayer Brings Answers

During prayer one morning I was prompted to pray for a woman of God who is very dear to me. As I quieted my spirit, I heard the Lord speak, "In Order to Survive the Storm, Sometimes You've Got to Get Out of the Boat." Immediately, the account of Peter "walking on the water" came to mind.

In the 14th chapter of Matthew verses 22-26: 'Jesus told His disciples to get into the boat and go ahead of Him to the other side while He sent away the crowd. After the multitudes of people were sent on their way, Jesus went up into the mountain alone to pray. The ship that the disciples were in that was now in the midst of the sea began to be tossed by the wind and the waves. As Jesus begun walking towards the disciples on water, they became troubled and cried out in fear because they thought He was a ghost.'[3]

"But straightway Jesus spake unto them, saying, 'Be of good cheer; it is I; be not afraid.' And Peter answered him and said, 'Lord, if it be thou, bid me come unto thee on the water.' And he said, 'Come.'"[4] 'Peter took a leap of faith, stepped out of the boat, and began walking towards Jesus on the water. While he was in the midst of walking toward Jesus on the water, Peter took his eyes off Jesus and He began to focus on what was going on around him.'[5]

'Frightened Peter cried out, "Lord, save me," because he began to sink.'[6] "And immediately Jesus stretched forth his hand... 'O thou of little faith, wherefore did you doubt?' And when they were come into the ship, the wind ceased."[7]

There will be times when a storm will hit your life and depending upon the size of the storm, sometimes it will rock your very foundation. It's what you do in the midst of the storm that will determine your outcome. Occasionally, Jesus will call you out of something and take you back to that very same thing to show not only you, but everyone with you, and even those that are no longer with you, that He is indeed the "Son of God." Are you willing to step outside of the boat?

> IT'S WHAT YOU DO IN THE MIDST OF THE STORM THAT WILL DETERMINE YOUR OUTCOME.

Today, if you have found yourself in the center of a storm and it feels as if the only way out is for you to step out on faith, then Jesus is talking to you. He's saying, "COME."[8] But you must stay focused because if you keep your eyes on Him, Jesus will be your anchor and you will not sink.

Pray the Prayer of Faith:

Father, today, I'm looking to YOU for direction and I am keeping my eyes on YOU. Although my way seems a little uncertain at this moment, I know that YOU will securely keep me safe within YOUR arms. Help me, Father God, to focus only on YOU and not on what I am going through. My hope and my trust are completely in YOU. In Jesus' Name, Amen.

CHAPTER TWO

What Comes to Mind When You Think About The Name, JESUS?

What comes to mind when you think about the name, "JESUS?" Is it: "give me, give me, give me?" Or is it "JESUS, what can I do for YOU?" God placed JESUS on this earth on purpose and for that very reason, God created you.

JESUS has carried out the plan God had for His life and is now sitting at the right hand of God the Father, interceding on your behalf. You are here in His stead for such a time as now. Have you chosen to do as JESUS did? Have you set out to accomplish the purpose for which you exist? Have you begun executing the plan God the Father has placed you on this earth to do? There are countless lives hanging in the balance. Limitless numbers of unfruitful people who can be considered dead men and women walking, all in need of their Master's touch.

Right now, there are people you know, individuals that will be connected to you for a lifetime, who are living in sin. Others will enter in your life and then exit from your life. Some will only come across your path for a season. Whatever the length of time, ALL of them have one need in common and His name is JESUS.

HAVE YOU BEGUN EXECUTING THE PLAN GOD THE FATHER HAS PLACED YOU ON THIS EARTH TO DO?

A number of them are in distress.

Some have no joy. Others are sick in their bodies. Many desire peace and are searching for direction. There are even cries for financial relief. God wants to totally deliver everyone out of his or her suffering and He's more than able and willing to do so!

You say ... "How can I help?" Well, I'm glad you asked; are you available to be His witness? We are given instruction in Galatians 6:1, the scripture reads, "Brethren, if a man be overtaken in a fault, ye which are spiritual, restore such an one in the spirit of meekness; considering thyself, lest thou also be tempted."[9] What this scripture conveys is if we see our brother or sister "overtaken" in any kind of wrongdoing - we who are spiritual (we who live by the spirit) - are to go to that person in love, telling him/her what is right so that he/she can be given the opportunity to make things right with God.[10] At the same time, we must be mindful of what is taking place so that we will not be tempted. After all, ... "For what is a man profited, if he shall gain the whole world, and lose his own soul? or what shall a man give in exchange for his soul?"[11]

God made a promise to man, and He vowed that, "If my people, which are called by my name, shall humble themselves, and pray, and seek my face, and turn from their wicked ways; then will I hear from heaven, and will forgive their sin, and will heal their land."[12]

Isaiah 55:3 says, "Incline your ear, and come unto me: hear, and your soul shall live; and I will make an everlasting covenant with you, even the sure mercies of David."[13] Here God summons the Christian believer to pay attention as He gives advice on righteous living. Then God vowed that whoever did these things He would make an "everlasting covenant" with them and also give to them His faithful love He promised David.[14] Now that's true covenant!

Pray the Prayer of Faith:

Father God in Heaven, I want to be more like Jesus. God, I pray that my life exemplifies my Lord and Savior Jesus Christ. Help me, Lord, to be the change YOU want to see in the world today. Help me to bring the truth to those who come across my path whether it's for a reason, a season, or a lifetime. God, YOU said that, "..man shall not live by bread alone, but by every word of God."[15] Father give me words of life to speak to those I minister to so that the words I release will lead them straight to YOU, they will receive from YOU and be delivered and set free in the Name of Jesus I pray and I count it done. Amen.

CHAPTER THREE

A Ripe Harvest

When Jesus represented God in the earth He went about teaching and preaching wherever God led Him. Jesus only taught and did what He learned from the Father and because of this, the "Power of God" was displayed mightily in His life throughout His entire ministry. There were miracles, signs and wonders that followed. The casting out of demonic forces was in full force. Diseased and sick bodies were healed in His name.

One day Jesus began talking to His disciples regarding the harvest of souls that were waiting to be brought into His kingdom.[16] "Then saith he unto his disciples, the harvest truly is plenteous, but the labourers are few..."[17] He encouraged His disciples to, "Pray ye therefore the Lord of the harvest, that he will send forth labourers into his harvest."[18]

Why are we not seeing an abundance of souls harvested in our land?[19] What happened to the power?

Large numbers of people are stressed, in distress, poverty stricken and in need of liberation. Many people desire healing and deliverance in their mind, body, and soul. Jesus' Heart was full of compassion for all who possessed the mindset and willingness to want to be saved, healed, delivered, and made whole by being set free from whatever held them captive. Everyone has been called to serve. It's not just the responsibility of the five-fold ministry gifts[20] to gather and call-in souls. You don't have to stand behind a pulpit to do it. Every man has been called to the ministry of reconciliation. The duty falls on every Christian—Believer after being saved, taught, and equipped with the Word of God—to go out into the field to teach and preach the "Good News" and win people to Christ. That's one of the ways God's Kingdom is built and established here on the earth. Are you willing to go?

EVERY MAN HAS BEEN CALLED TO THE MINISTRY OF RECONCILIATION.

In the Holy Bible Matthew 9:35-38 records, "And Jesus went about all the cities and villages, teaching in their synagogues, and preaching the gospel of the kingdom, and healing every sickness and every disease among the people. But when he saw the multitudes, he was moved with compassion on them, because they fainted, and were scattered abroad, as sheep having no shepherd. Then saith he unto his disciples, The harvest truly is plenteous, but the labourers are few; pray ye therefore the

Lord of the harvest, that he will send forth labourers into his harvest."[21]

Jesus prepared the disciples before they were sent and equipped them with supernatural power. Acts 1:8 speaks of this power given by God through the Holy Spirit.[22] The scripture reads "But ye shall receive power, after that the Holy Ghost is come upon you: and ye shall be witnesses unto me both in Jerusalem, and in all Judea, and in Samaria, and unto the uttermost part of the earth."[23]

Jesus was committed to the Father, His work and His Word. Jesus was sent into the earth to accomplish the will of the Father. He was concerned about God's harvest, and He remained faithful and committed to be a harvester of souls all the way to the grave. You were sent into the earth for that very same purpose. Will you, "Pray ye therefore the Lord of the harvest, that he will send forth labourers into his harvest?"[24] Better yet will you go, too?

Pray the Prayer of Faith:

Heavenly Father, it is my prayer that YOU give me the same compassion that is entrenched within YOUR Heart. Lord I come boldly yet humbly asking YOU, Father to send forth YOUR labourers to harvest YOUR field to do YOUR Will.[25] I understand and know YOU have called everyone to the ministry of reconciliation and I promise to do my part. Send me, I'll go. I will do YOUR Will. And when I go let them only see YOU. Kingdom of God come, Will of God be done in and through my life while I am serving YOU here in the earth. In Jesus' Name I pray. Amen.

CHAPTER FOUR

Doing Things God's Way

In the life of every believer obeying God isn't optional, it is essential! Obeying God always take precedence over any other way. There will always be other available options on how things should and need to be done, but the reality of it all is there's only one right way to get it done and that's "Doing It God's Way." God didn't leave us clueless as it relates to how to get things done. In fact, God sent us an example to show us and then left an instruction manual behind in the form of the Holy Bible.

God chose to send His "only begotten Son"[26], Jesus, into this world before we entered into time, to save us from a lifetime of sin and self-destruction. What a selfless, loving, and gracious God He is to send His only Son, Jesus, into the earth whom later He would use as a sacrifice to demonstrate for us exactly how He wanted us to live. "What is man, that thou art mindful of him? And the son of man, that thou visitest him. For thou hast made him a little lower than the angels, and hast crowned him with glory and honour. Thou madest him to have dominion over the works of thy hands; thou hast put all things under his feet..."[27] God has given man (genderless) the liberty to choose what he/she does in life; He has already established a plan and a purpose for the life of man's existence in the earth.

HAVE YOU BEGUN EXECUTING THE PLAN GOD THE FATHER HAS PLACED YOU ON THIS EARTH TO DO?

For over 2000 years, man has been walking in disobedience to the Will of the Father. And because of man's reasoning he has given more thought to what he/she wants. When we think of ourselves higher than we ought, we unwisely resist from counting the cost, and we typically choose our way over God's.

More often than not man continues to reap an unwanted harvest for not giving serious thought to what the outcome will be stemming from the choices he/she has made. With no regard to the effects it will have on those to whom we are connected, our decisions sometimes yield a grave consequence.

If there wasn't a need for God to send Jesus into the world, God would not have sent Him. But God saw that there was a solemn need for man's deliverance and well-being. Man was in definite need of a Savior, a Redeemer, One who could not only rescue him from a burning hell, but also from a life of total destruction.

God chose to send the Ultimate One who would bring total restoration to the spirit of man, mind, body, and soul resulting in man living life in eternity. Jesus allowed the Father to occupy every area of His life willingly. Jesus gave God the freedom to rule and reign in His life no matter the cost. Literally, physically, and uncompromisingly, Jesus died to self, doing the Will of the Father; Jesus died a selfless death. "For he hath made him to be sin for us, who knew no sin: that we might be made the righteousness of God in him."[28]

As I gave way to the voice of the Holy Spirit in the middle of writing a song that I remembered hearing many times during my adolescent years resonated in my spirit. So decided to do a little research in regard to what I'd heard. I found within the words that were echoed throughout this particular song that it left no room for doubt in my mind that the life this individual sung about depicted the very image of how this person both saw and lived life.

Two scriptures pertaining to obedience flowed through my spirit: 1 Samuel 15:22, "Wouldn't it be far better to obey than to sacrifice?"[29] and Matthew 16:24, "Then said Jesus unto his disciples, If any man will come after me, let him deny himself, and take up his cross, and follow me."[30]

It doesn't take a rocket scientist to figure out that God didn't send us a Leader in the form of Jesus the Christ just for us to lead ourselves and be guided by fleshly desires. God intentionally sent Jesus into the earth to be an illustration to all how life ought to be lived. As a result of coming to know God the Father through a personal intimate relationship with Jesus; God made it accessible for every man to tap into the purpose and plan God specifically designed for his life. It's a simple formula. Total Surrender + Total Submission = Completely Dying to Self. This equation will always be a winning combination! When man recognizes that not every plan of his is a plan of God's, his plans will succeed every time.

Pray the Prayer of Faith

Heavenly Father, Thank YOU for helping me to clearly see the purpose and the plan for which YOU have made me. Help me, oh God, to commit all the works of my hands unto YOU so that I will only commit to doing only the things YOU have planned for me to do. I surrender myself to YOU, Lord, so that the plans YOU have for me will succeed. I yield my spirit, body, mind, and soul; have YOUR way in me. I desire to walk in total obedience to YOUR Will for my life, and I submit to YOUR way. Lord, I give YOU my heart. In the matchless Name of Jesus, I pray. Amen.

CHAPTER FIVE

At Midnight

"And at midnight Paul and Silas prayed, and sang praises unto God: and the prisoners heard them."[31]

In the Book of Acts, 'Paul and Silas found themselves incarcerated not because of the wrong they had done but because of the stance they took in Christ. After being bound by chains, beaten, and thrown into prison, both Paul and Silas decided not to become disheartened and discouraged but they chose to pray and sing praises unto God.'[32] These fearless men chose not to the let situation cause them to murmur and complain. As an alternative, Paul and Silas had a made-up mind to call on the God they knew and wait for Him to deliver them from what temporarily detained them physically. Despite the fact of being imprisoned in the flesh, they refused to let the burden of being locked up enslave them mentally, emotionally, or spiritually.

Both Paul and Silas could have become troubled and bitter because serving Christ positioned them in jail. Instead, they chose to agree together in prayer, asking God to support and comfort them in the midst of difficulty. Comprised within their request was for God to visit them and be with them in prison just like He was with Joseph. They also petitioned God to visit them in prison as they prayed that the consolation of Christ might abound, as their suffering for Him did.[33]

...THEIR PLEA WAS ALSO FOR GOD TO FORGIVE THEIR PERSECUTORS...

Even though the beating Paul and Silas received left them bruised and in pain, neither one of them prayed a self-centered prayer. Praise went up on behalf of what they unjustly received. They wanted everything they experienced to, in some way, further the gospel. Their appeal to God was not only for deliverance, but their plea was also for God to forgive their persecutors and turn their hearts towards Him.

Right in the middle of their pain and unwarranted imprisonment both Paul and Silas possessed an attitude of gratitude in spite of the lot that had befallen them. They were confident that the same God who gave them solace and brought relief to their pain was the very same God who was able free them, too.

As Paul and Silas prayed and continued to sing praises unto God at midnight,[34] God met them in the middle of their affliction and delivered them out of the hands of their enemies.

Therefore, it does not matter what predicament you have been placed in. I encourage you to pray and to sing praises unto God wherever your stance for God has seated you. Whatever your midnight may be, if you would just lift your heart up to God and cry out to Him, He will come exactly where you are and do for you whatever it is that you need Him to do.

Never allow the sufferings of this present world to grip you to the point that it renders you powerless and causes you to be incapable of praying and singing praises to God. Cry aloud, spare not, lift up your voice like a trumpet, and count yourself worthy to suffer shame for Jesus' Name. You can't wait until the battle is over, shout in the victory.

Pray the Prayer of Faith

Father God, I am so glad that YOU call me friend because YOU are, "...a friend that sticketh closer than a brother." [35] *I worship and adore YOU. I totally depend on YOU to give me exactly what I need. As I take my stance in this hard place (insert concern), it's good to know that YOU are right here with me. Thank YOU, God for inspiring the writers of old to pen YOUR Heart concerning me. I place my life in YOUR hands. Thank YOU, Lord for giving me everything that I need that pertains to life and godliness. I will shout in victory now while I wait for my change to come. In Jesus' Name I pray. Amen.*

CHAPTER SIX

From Unforgiveness to Forgiveness...

Rx: Until Seventy x Seven

Thanks be to God there are no disadvantages when it comes to forgiveness. Forgiveness breeds good health benefits with no adverse side effects. The downside to being unable to forgive places a person with an unforgiving heart at risk in his/her relationship with God. Unforgiveness always makes the situation worse because the individual becomes bitter leaving the person walking in offense in a critical state.

Unforgiveness is like a cancer...it eats away at you. It robs you of your inner peace putting undue stress on your body physically. You become emotionally unstable and mentally unsettled. Refusal to forgive can cause severe harm in the life of the person who has decided not to give it. The end result boils down to not being able to walk in unconditional love, which is the God-kind of love.

If you are dealing with unforgiveness, it must be recognized because it is a trick of the enemy; solely designed to make you walk outside of the Will of God. Walking outside the Will of God will hinder you from reaching your destiny.

In Matthew 18: 21-23, Peter asked Jesus a question.[36] When Jesus answered, he left no room for assumption. "Then came Peter to him, and said, Lord, how oft shall my brother sin against me, and I forgive him? Till seven times? Jesus saith unto him, I say not unto thee, Until seven times: but, Until seventy times seven."[37] If you haven't already at some point in your life had the need to forgive someone for something that they said or done to you, before you leave this earth you will be faced with the decision to forgive. Forgive, "What does it mean to forgive?" Forgiving simply is the ability to release anyone from the hurt and or grieve that they have caused you.

WALKING OUTSIDE THE WILL OF GOD WILL HINDER YOU FROM REACHING YOUR DESTINY.

Every believing heart should possess the same compassion that God has extended to them towards another. If anyone has wronged you, you should extend the same forgiveness that God gave to you in order that you may forgive whoever has mistreated you in any way. To those whom forgiveness is given, forgiveness is also required. There are NO exceptions to this rule! No one is exempt. What this specifies is that forgiveness is a requirement not for some but for everyone who receives it. Forgiveness is a choice that must be independently made by all.

In Matthew chapter 18, a story is told of a king who wanted to settle accounts with his servants.[38]

"Therefore is the kingdom of heaven likened unto a certain king, which would take account of his servants. And when he had begun to reckon, one was brought unto him, which owed him ten thousand talents. But forasmuch as he had not to pay, his lord commanded him to be sold, and his wife, and children, and all that he had, and payment to be made. The servant therefore fell down, and worshipped him, saying, Lord, have patience with me, and I will pay thee all. Then the lord of that servant was moved with compassion, and loosed him, and forgave him the debt. But the same servant went out, and found one of his fellowservants, which owed him an hundred pence: and he laid hands on him, and took him by the throat, saying, Pay me that thou owest. And his fellowservant fell down at his feet, and besought him, saying, Have patience with me, and I will pay thee all. And he would not: but went and cast him into prison, till he should pay the debt. So when his fellowservants saw what was done, they were very sorry, and came and told unto their lord all that was done. Then his lord, after that he had called him, said unto him, O thou wicked servant, I forgave thee all that debt, because thou desiredst me:

shouldest not thou also have had compassion on thy fellowservant, even as I had pity on thee?

And his lord was wroth, and delivered him to the tormentors, till he should pay all that was due unto him."[39]

Although forgiving all may be a hard pill to swallow, it's the medicine that the DOCTOR ordered. If you take it with a dose of "I can do all things through Christ which strengtheneth me..."[40] it will make the pill a lot easier to swallow when it's your turn to take it.

Unforgiveness does not come in a certain size, shape, or color. It does not matter whether it's old or new. It has no boundaries. Its perimeters can be wide, far reaching and its wounds sometimes run deep; but forgiveness is necessary. Don't allow unforgiveness to take up residence in your heart. Freedom comes only after you forgive. Release whoever has wronged you so you can love unconditionally. That is the GOD kind of love we are called to live out.

Pray the Prayer of Faith

Father, help me to clear my conscience of offense. Just as YOU have forgiven me, I must forgive too.[41] When I experience injustice, help me, oh God, to freely forgive as YOU have freely forgiven me. A true believer's heart must not hold grudges or become bitter but must show unconditional love. God, I thank YOU for loving me enough that YOUR conviction floods my spirit. I desire to have a loving heart like YOU so I can forgive instantly like YOU did. I will be a living example of what a heart of forgiveness is supposed to be. Use me for YOUR glory King Jesus, in the name of Jesus I pray. Amen.

CHAPTER SEVEN

No More Excuses

The day I heard the words "No More Excuses" I sat yielded waiting to pen God's Heart. The sound of stillness infiltrated the room. I didn't try to rush things; I just continued to sit in His Presence while waiting for the Lord's release. It was not until the Lord knew He had my undivided attention that He had me write what He was saying through these three words to me... "No More Excuses." Soon after, the Lord began to minister to me... "I hear you saying that you're waiting on ME. But what have I been telling you to do that you have yet to accomplish for ME? It's not that you are not fully equipped with what you need to get the job done. It's just that your faith has left you challenged—that's why you haven't begun. I have provided within you everything you need. I know what you can do. I put it in you. If you use what I have already given you, then you have my permission to proceed."

I sat there after writing what I'd just heard with my mind in deep thought thinking, *"Lord where are You taking me?"* This is extremely different from all the other things I have previously written. It was then that God reminded me of how I always ask Him to allow me to pen "His Heart" for "The Hearer."

God led me to 2 Peter 1. There in the scriptures, it is written that "God" gave Jesus power, and with that same power you were given everything you need to live here in the earth and to serve God. The reason you have been given these things is because you know Jesus. Jesus called you by His glory and His goodness. Through His glory and His goodness, Jesus gave to you great and precious promises. God wanted you to partake in His character so that the world would not ruin you with its wickedness and deceitfulness.[42]

GOD WANTED YOU TO PARTAKE IN HIS CHARACTER SO THAT THE WORLD WOULD NOT RUIN YOU WITH ITS WICKEDNESS AND DECEITFULNESS.

The Lord continued, I have given you "ME." "NO MORE EXCUSES." Just trust Me. The Holy Spirit was sent to lead and guide you. You are secure because I AM with you. Therefore, move forward. You've been equipped with what I have placed on the inside of you.

Doesn't My Word declare that "The steps of a good man are ordered by the Lord..."[43] I have pre-planned it all. You can move forward in My confidence and with My assurance.

"NO MORE EXCUSES" is what I kept hearing God say, and I know this may sound poetic but it's prophetic; so, hear the Word of the Lord spoken to you today. I'm sharing this portion of God's Message, my testimony to let you know that God assured you when He called you that He would supply your every need. God promised that He would be with you until the end of time. However, there are some things that you must first do before God fulfills the plans He has for you. God is 100% committed and you must be 100% committed too. When you do your part, it obligates God to do His part. Therefore, the next time God gives you instructions and your mind tries to give you excuses telling you that you're waiting on Him, look back over your life, beloved, to see if you have completed everything God has required of you. In doing so, you may find that the delay could possibly be that God is waiting on you to do something that you should have already done.

Pray the Prayer of Faith

Most gracious and all wise God, before I was born, You charted the course for my life. I know YOU say in your Word, "For I know the thoughts that I think toward you, saith the Lord, thoughts of peace, and not of evil, to give you an expected end."[44] YOUR Word says that YOU have already given me everything "...that pertain to life and godliness."[45] Knowing this, I know I already have what I need. Therefore God, I'm asking YOU to reveal to me the areas in my life where I have fallen short, and I have not done what YOU have required of me. Here I am, Lord. I'm seeking YOUR face. Help me, oh God, to rid my life of all excuses. I want to live a life that is pleasing in YOUR sight. I want to be used by YOU. I aspire and I long to live the life YOU have already pre-planned for me. I thank YOU, Lord, for revealing where I have been slothful so that I will see and carry out all the things that I am responsible for doing. I Thank YOU for giving me grace, and for patiently waiting on me. I love YOU, Lord. YOU will get the glory out of my life in Jesus' Name I pray, Amen.

CHAPTER EIGHT

NEVER Late...

ALWAYS On Time

This book is a byproduct of a blog I created in November of 2011. I was sitting at my desk on October 31st to be exact when the Lord dropped the word AIM in my spirit. I remember immediately picking up my memo pad and writing it down. When I took note of what I'd written the words "An Inspiring Moment" leaped off the paper.

That same day I sent out an inspirational email to the contacts listed in my email account and entitled it *AIM...An Inspiring Moment with Kim Holmes*. Two weeks later, the blog came into existence.

At the dawning of each day, I began to posture myself to hear from the Lord before sending out the message He would place in my spirit for AIM that day. Upon awakening one Wednesday morning it sounded as if someone turned the radio on high volume. Repeatedly the lyrics played nonstop over and over again in my head. The song I was hearing blessed my soul because I could attest to the fact of how great God really is. I rested in what I was hearing and continued the routine of my morning with the exception of sending out AIM. It wasn't until after I made my regular stop that I realized why AIM did not get sent out; God was in the process of shifting An Inspiring Moment.

Upon entering the store there was a song playing on the radio. This wasn't unusual because this particular store always played music. I proceeded to get my coffee continuing to listen the artist. Upon sitting my cup down on the counter my mind was taken back to the lyrics that

GOD IS GREATER THAN YOUR PROBLEM.

were present in my spirit before my feet hit the floor. At that very moment I knew God had placed a specific word in my spirit that He wanted to be released on that day.

I paid for my coffee, returned to my vehicle, and I positioned myself to hear God's heart for the recipients of AIM. As I drove to work, my spirit—man began speaking. I grabbed my phone and began recording 99.9 percent of what you are about to read.

I don't know what situation that you are currently facing or what circumstances you presently find yourself in. But there is one thing I do know and that is God is greater than your problem. He is greater than anything that you are experiencing at this point in your life. Whether you are being attacked in your body and you're in need of healing, God is the "Great Physician." He can totally heal and deliver you; setting you free from the sickness that is trying to destroy your health if you would just take Him at His word and trust Him.

Maybe today you're in a financial crisis and you don't know which way to turn. God is Greater than your bank account. I'm here to tell you that although you find yourself in a tight place, you've got to know that God is Greater than your own state of affairs.

The loved ones that have been weighing heavy on your heart; God is Greater than their sin and He can save them, too. Didn't God save you?

Perhaps you're at a crossroads and you need clarity on the next move you are about to make. You know that it's imperative that you not make the wrong decision because it not only involves you, but the lives of your family members, too. Can I tell you that if you would just seek the Face of God, you will find the answer to the question(s) you are searching for.

Yes!!! God is Great!!! He is Greater than your yesterday, He is Greater than your today, and He is Greater than your tomorrow!

So, if you've reached the point where you need relief whether it be for healing, deliverance, finances, loved ones, direction; whatever your need is today, God is the answer.

There's NO need to look any further because there is a "balm in Gilead"[46] that can bring healing to your soul. My recommendation is that you apply the healing balm directly to that specific need in your life. "In everything give thanks: for this is the will of God in Christ Jesus concerning you."[47]

Pray the Prayer of Faith

Father God, right now I touch and agree with every man, woman, boy or girl that is praying this prayer at this very moment. God, YOU know what it is that they stand in need of. God, we are, "...looking unto Jesus the author and finisher of our faith..."[48] God, YOU know where they are. YOUR Word says that "...if I make my bed in hell, behold, thou art there."[49] So, right now Father, in the Name of Jesus, I come against the very thing that has been trying to make them doubt that they are not coming out. God bring to them sweet relief and settle their account today. I speak to their spirit—man and I say arise because you have now come out of what has been trying to make you weary in well doing. Today, God, the Balm of Gilead[50], is applied to your situation in the Name of Jesus. I prophesy and I speak directly to the names of sickness, financial lack, unsaved loved ones. Bring clarity and peace to whatever they may be faced with today, God. I thank YOU for setting them at liberty. God, I declare and decree and pronounce that the blessings needed have been released into their lives because YOU have not only given them liberty, but YOU have given them the victory in Christ Jesus. Amen and Amen!

CHAPTER NINE

We Must Consider Our Ways

"Now therefore thus saith the Lord of hosts; 'Consider your ways.'"[51]

Countless numbers of people live their life today indulging in self-gratification. Some of them are of the mindset that they can do whatever they want and for however long they want. While there may be some validity to this utterance due to freewill given to the individual, the consequences of one's choices can be very costly.

When we look at the grand scope of things the reality of it all is tomorrow isn't promised to anyone. The decision to continue in sin leaves a person in a critical state. The sad news is this is not only the thought pattern of the unsaved. Can we be real? There are many in the Church today serving in various positions from the pulpit to the door that have opted to live a life of pleasure-seeking. However, this earthly mindset leads them down the path of destruction.

Romans 12 gives explicit instructions on how the Christian Believer ought to present him/herself. It is not realistic to live like the world day to day, then show up at Church on Sunday morning, during mid- week services, special events and sit in any position as if the life lived the entire week represented the kingdom. It does not matter what chair you occupy. To the preacher, the teacher, the one who prays or prophecies in Jesus' Name.

To the praise and worship leader and the team; to the one who is lifting up your voice and hands in praise and worship, too. To the one standing to bear witness to the Word by saying amen; to the one that serves in any capacity; even to the one who just sits in the pew, the Holy Spirit is talking to you. "...God is not mocked..."[52] No Sir! No Ma'am! Living with this type of immoral behavior is simply forbidden.

NOTHING IS EVER HIDDEN FROM GOD'S VIEW.

It's full of deceitfulness and involves covering up while wallowing in sin. Nothing is ever hidden from God's view. There will be a public reward for what is done in private.

"But all things that are reproved are made manifest by the light: for whatsoever doth make manifest is light."[53] Pretense will never exchange places with godliness. There's a penalty to be paid for having no remorse.

God is to be worshiped "in spirit and in truth."[54] "No man can serve two masters: for either he will hate the one and love the other. It is time for those who are of the household of faith to stand up for God and His righteousness."[55] Stop the horseplay. 'No more bearing false witness.'[56] Surrender all and submit to the King of Kings. Commit to a lifestyle of holiness. Rise up People of God and stop playing Church and become the Church. For God says, "Be ye holy; for I am holy."[57] Are you in?

My brothers, my sisters what we do and say as Children of God counts. I can't stress it enough, "...Consider your ways."[58]

2 Corinthians 5:15 serves as a reminder why the Son of God was crucified, died, and rose again.

"...that he died for all, that they which live should not henceforth live unto themselves, but unto him which died for them, and rose again. Wherefore henceforth know we no man after the flesh: yea, though we have known Christ after the flesh, yet now henceforth know we him no more. Therefore, if any man be in Christ, he is a new creature: old things are passed away; behold, all things are become new."[59] We must consider our ways and there is just no way around it because God is not the only one who is watching.

Pray the Prayer of Faith

Father, today I come to YOU as humbly as I know how. First of all, thanking YOU for keeping me (even while I was straddling the fence) with one foot in the kingdom and the other foot out while YOU still covered me. Thank YOU, God, for patiently waiting on me even when I knew better and still yielded to my flesh. God, YOU loved me even in my unlovable state. YOU watched over me, cared for me, and protected me. Thank YOU for loving me beyond me. I could have been dead sleeping in my grave, but YOU chose not to let me die in my sin. Thank you for providing a way of escape for me. I'm grateful for YOUR unconditional love. I renounce my sin (name it) and I surrender and turn my life over to YOU every day, in every way. I freely give YOU me for the rest of my life and I choose to live solely for YOU. In Jesus' Name I pray, Amen.

CHAPTER TEN

WARNING:

Your Own Tongue Can

Become Your

Worst Enemy

Words are the one thing that you can't take back once they are released. Words will have a positive or negative flow in our life, as well as, in the lives of those to whom they're addressed. Therefore, we need to be cognizant of the language we use when we speak. Words are so powerful that they can assist in healing and deliverance. Or words will destroy and bring disaster to the life of an individual causing heartache, pain, and misery.

If we are not careful, inappropriate words will rob a person of their inner peace by stealing their joy adding stress; a weight that could only grow to become very heavy. We must not forget, "Death and life are in the power of the tongue: and they that love it shall eat the fruit thereof."[60] We need to be mindful of the words we use as well as the reason for using them. Words help to shape our lives. Words form images in our minds. Our life will turn out to be a carbon copy of that which we verbalize. This is why so many people constantly take trips back to those uncomfortable, overwhelming places in their lives. Don't allow your own tongue to become your worst enemy.

OUR LIFE WILL TURN OUT TO BE A CARBON COPY OF THAT WHICH WE VERBALIZE.

By chance if these words have penetrated you to the very core of your mind, I ask that you take inventory.

Find a place where you can get alone with God; a place where no interruptions will occur. Re-examine what you have been saying. Take this time to reflect upon the words you have been releasing. Have useless words gotten into your head? Through reassessment, God will make known to you what has been hindering and/or blocking you.

Words do have a boomerang effect—finding its way back to the one who possesses ownership. Don't allow your words to walk all over you.

"Even so the tongue is a little member, and boasteth great things. Behold, how great a matter a little fire kindleth! And the tongue is a fire, a world of iniquity: so is the tongue among our members, that it defileth the whole body, and setteth on fire the course of nature; and it is set on fire of hell. For every kind of beasts, and of birds, and of serpents, and of things in the sea, is tamed, and hath been tamed of mankind: but the tongue can no man tame; it is an unruly evil, full of deadly poison. Therewith bless we God, even the Father; and therewith curse we men, which are made after the similitude of God. Out of the same mouth proceedeth blessing and cursing. My brethren, these things ought not so to be."[61]

Make conscience decisions to speak with seasoned words daily; words that possess the power to propel you forward, not leave you behind.

Pray the Prayer of Faith

Father, today I place my tongue in YOUR hands. Lord Jesus, help me to speak only the words I need to speak. I need YOU to take over my mind. Give me YOUR thoughts to speak so that I will refrain from saying negative, hurtful, and harmful things. Speak through me, Lord, when I open my mouth. I need my words to be seasoned in order to release what will be pleasing to YOU, words that will not hold me back from moving forward. In Jesus' Name I pray. Amen.

CHAPTER ELEVEN

Leave the Past in the Past

Why choose to be stuck in yesterday? Yesterday is gone and a new day has come. Holding onto things from the past; wasting precious time dealing with useless stuff—don't allow yourself to stay in an undesirable place for too long. See it as a steppingstone, not a stumbling block and move on.

Learn from the experience and let go so you can grow. Trials didn't come to last, only to make you stronger. You can make it through the process. You've just got to hang in there because you were built to weather any storm. What you have encountered has come to test your faith. 'You've already been given everything you need to continue to run this race.'[62] "But let patience have her perfect work, that ye may be perfect and entire, wanting nothing."[63]

Talk to God. He will instruct you and give you wisdom to guide you through. Do only the things that He tells you to do. Then God will give you your breakthrough. We are assured in HIS WORD that, "God is not a man, that he should lie; neither the son of man, that he should repent: hath he said, and shall he not do it? or hath he spoken, and shall he not make it good?"[64] 'God's word will never return void!'[65]

Beloved, you don't have to live in yesterday! You can move forward with grace and in the peace of God. Expect God to do it. Don't "waver" in doubt.[66] God is more than able to do what you have asked Him to do. Just believe that you have already received what you have asked for.

DO ONLY THE THINGS THAT HE TELLS YOU TO DO.

My friend, you've come this far by faith; now allow faith to take you the rest of the way. Be persistent. Stay consistent. Have patience and worship while you wait. You will be blessed far more than you have ever imagined, believed, or dreamed of, after you have succeeded in passing the test.

James writes in 1:2-8, 12, "My brethren, count it all joy when ye fall into diverse temptations; knowing this, that the trying of your faith worketh patience. But let patience have her perfect work, that ye may be perfect and entire, wanting nothing. If any of you lack wisdom, let him ask of God, that giveth to all men liberally, and upbraideth not; and it shall be given him. But let him ask in faith, nothing wavering. For he that wavereth is like a wave of the sea driven with the wind and tossed. For let not that man think that he shall receive any thing of the Lord. A double minded man is unstable in all his ways...Blessed is the man that endureth temptation: for when he is tried, he shall receive the crown of life, which the Lord hath promised to them that love him."[67]

Pray the Prayer of Faith

Father God in the Name of Jesus, first of all I give you praise. It is because of YOU that I'm able to "...run with patience the race that is set before us."[68] God, I thank YOU for YOUR assistance during the testing of my faith. Thank YOU for being my help. God, I ask YOU to tell me everything I need to do in order to make it through this trying time. I'm ready to move from yesterday. I am ready to leave the past in the past. I will stay the course until my breakthrough comes. Thank YOU for YOUR wisdom and for YOUR strength day by day. I will push my way through this trial into victory. In Jesus' Name I pray. Amen.

CHAPTER TWELVE

What do YOU do When the Issue is YOU...?

David simply was 'a man after God's own heart.'[69] Even though he was greatly used by God, David had some private issues which caused him to have some serious encounters with God because he had to face the consequences of his actions. Some of the matters David had to confront and conquer were self-inflicted due to his desire to fulfill the lusts of his flesh. For that reason, sin entered his life through the door he opened. What gave David pleasures for a season later inflicted great pain upon him, due to the choices he made.

Nevertheless, David's inadequacies caused him to reach for God and not run from him. On many occasions his shortcomings lead him straight to repentance. Despite the fact that there were many times David got out of alignment with the Will of God, David never allowed what he had done in the past to affect the outcome of who God said that he would later become. David always had a heart to serve and please God.

And as a result of his strong desire to be a God—pleaser, David sought the Lord, knowing that there would be a hefty price he had to pay because of his craving to fulfill the lusts of his flesh. He never tried to disown what he'd done, nor did he wait for anyone to tell him of his need to repent. 'David just fell on his face and wept before the Lord when he was convicted, asked for forgiveness from his immorality and every time our merciful loving God heard his sincere cry, He forgave him for what he had done. By owning up to his sins, David chose to face God's correction and dealt with the lot given him.'[70]

GOD IS EAGER TO HEAL AND DELIVER YOU RIGHT WHERE YOU ARE. HIS FORGIVENESS IS INSTANT.

Just as in the days of old, the same is still happening in this world today. People are running rampant fulfilling their earthly desires, and not counting the cost. Some are hurting, killing, misusing and abusing people with their tongues while others are doing the same but using physical force. At the hands of the selfish inhabitants in this land, lives are being and have become emotional wrecks. Due to being emotionally, physically, mentally, and spiritually challenged, many lives are being destroyed. It's simply a heart issue due to self-centeredness and godless living.

When your heart is not right, the things you do and say won't be right either. We find in Proverbs 3: 6-12 these admonitions: "In all thy ways acknowledge him, and he shall direct thy paths. Be not wise in thine own eyes: fear the Lord, and depart from evil...My son, despise not the chastening of the Lord; neither be weary of his correction: for whom the Lord loveth he correcteth; even as a father the son in whom he delighteth."[71] It's when we do not have reverence for God that we are destined to fall prey to the enemy.

Every person knows when they have done something wrong. At the onset of conviction, repentance needs to take place so that things can be made right between God and the individual. But are we, as kingdom people, really reverencing God? Are we falling on our faces and seeking God's mercy and grace for the wrong we have done that has displeased Him? Is searching your heart a part of your daily regimen?

If you find that you keep stumbling into issue after issue, it's time for a heart check. There is something that is preventing you from becoming all that God wants you to be. Why is it that you continuously fall short? Today I challenge you to take a good look inside your heart to see what's hidden within its walls that has been hindering you from walking in the fullness of your God-given potential.

No one should have to ever tell you that you need to ask for forgiveness especially when you confess that Jesus is Lord. No one should ever have to be pumped or primed to go independently before the Lord on their own, fall on their face and repent when their actions have called for penitence.

Beloved, the condition of your heart does matter! Your heart is the birthplace for godly increase not sinful desires. The Holy Bible tells us to pay attention to God's Word and not to let it out of our sight. 'It reminds us to keep God's Word in our hearts because it is life to anyone who finds it.'[72] These words assist us in maintaining our spiritual walk with God by showing us the way that leads to eternity. The Bible speaks saying: "...my words...For they are life unto those that find them, and health to all their flesh. Keep thy heart with all diligence; for out of it are the issues of life. Put away from thee a froward mouth, and perverse lips put far from thee. Let thine eyes look right on and let thine eyelids look straight before thee."[73] Always pursue holiness while paying close attention to following the path of peace and at the same time dedicating yourself to God in order that you may be able to refrain from evil in conversation and deed.

The seeds that you sow today will in no doubt produce tomorrow's harvest. You can avoid the pitfalls of being entangled in the yoke of bondage if you choose to live a God-conscious life on a daily basis. It's vital that you live a consecrated life every day.

Let's review *"What do you do when you don't have anyone to blame because the issue ... IS YOU?"* I'm glad you asked. It is simple: REPENT and be freed!

So, what does it mean to repent? To repent basically means that you have recognized the wrong that you have done, you are sorry and now you are ready to change your ways. Once this is done, transformation can begin to take place within your heart, and you are on your way to a reformed life. Although you may still feel the after-effects felt from the self-inflicted wounds, God is eager to heal and deliver you right where you are. His forgiveness is instant.

Child of God, every day I pray a simple but effective prayer and it goes like this "God when I get ready to say or do something that's out of YOUR character, please convict me on the spot." This simple but profound prayer keeps me rooted and grounded; and for that I'm grateful.

Proverbs 4:20-27 gives directives on how to make sure the issue can exclude you: "My son, attend to my words; incline thine ear unto my sayings. Let them not depart from thine eyes; keep them in the midst of thine heart. For they are life unto those that find them, and health to all their flesh. Keep thy heart with all diligence; for out of it are the issues of life. Put away from thee a froward mouth, and perverse lips put far from thee. Let thine eyes look right on and let thine eyelids look straight before thee. Ponder the path of thy feet and let all thy ways be established. Turn not to the right hand nor to the left: remove thy foot from evil."[74]

God is waiting to forgive you. Just come to God with a sincere heart, repent and 'God will freely pardon and remember the sin no more.'[75] Notice the "your" is no longer in front of sin. It's never too late for you to turn to the Lord.

As you were reading, if the words written began to leap off the pages, then the Holy Spirit is talking to you. My friend, the issue no longer has to be you.

Pray the Prayer of Faith

Father, it is in the Name of Jesus that I come to you with a heart of thanksgiving and my mouth filled with praise and honor today.[76] Thank YOU for loving me unconditionally even in my sin. Father, I come to you today on my own seeking total forgiveness from you today. I want to be freed from me. I need to be healed, I need to be delivered, and I need to be set free. God, I believe YOUR Word; therefore, I trust YOU by faith. YOUR WORD declares: "For I know the thoughts that I think toward you, saith the Lord, thoughts of peace, and not of evil, to give you and expected end."[77] Dear Lord, please forgive me (personally tell the Lord what you are repenting for). I am sorry for yielding to my flesh. Thank you for healing, delivering, and setting me free. I yield to the "...fruit of The Spirit... temperance"[78] and I give way for it to operate effectively in my life in the Name of Jesus. Lord Jesus have your way in me. Thank YOU, heavenly Father, for operating in me so that my words and actions will please YOU. Now God, as a sign of YOUR covenant promise, I seal this binding agreement to save, heal, deliver, and set free in Jesus' Name. Thank YOU for reforming my life. I am grateful because YOU have already begun the transformation process in my heart. In the Precious Name of YOUR Son Jesus the Christ, Son of the Living God, I pray Amen.

CHAPTER THIRTEEN

You Owe God Praise

Presently, at this moment if you do not have everything that you desire, still... "You Owe God Praise!" It was God's Hand of love that reached down and touched you and upon His Stroke, your eyes opened before rising... "What was the first thing you did?" You looked up. This was no coincidence. For this... "You Owe God Praise!"

God woke you up this morning giving you a fresh start to another day. God didn't only wake you up, 'He gave you grace and mercy to follow you throughout this day'[79] and because of this... "You Owe God Praise!"

Had it not been for God keeping your blood running warm through your veins as you slept...you would not have heard the alarm clock this morning. For this too... "You Owe God Praise!"

If you are of the mindset that it was your alarm clock that awakened you today, what about the morning the power went out and you woke up anyway? Who gets the praise? Think about it... "You Owe God Praise!"

YOU GET TO TELL THE STORY BUT WHO GETS THE GLORY? YOU OWE GOD PRAISE!

How about the job interview you went on yesterday? Today you're in high spirits because the employer gave you the job. It wasn't because you looked the part, nor was it your skill set or expertise. It was God's Voice inside the mind of the interviewer that told him/her to employ you. And for this... "You Owe God Praise!"

The school exam you took not knowing what the final outcome would be. You waited assuming you did make the grade because you labored in study late the previous night well into the next day. When the grades came in, you rushed to check and see how you did which confirmed what you already knew. You aced the exam like you thought you would. Who gave you the knowledge, understanding and wisdom to apply what you learned...? That's right... "You Owe God Praise!"

That car accident should have taken your life, but the fact of the matter is, you are still here, and your life was spared. Who saved you...? Yes you... "You Owe God Praise!"

You were diagnosed with an illness that you had never heard of before. You took test after test. You saw many different doctors and the doctors could not give you any answers for the diagnosis they gave. Then, all of a sudden, one night out of the blue all the symptoms left you. The pain that you felt was no longer on the inside of you. You went back to the doctor only to discover that the condition was miraculously gone. In the middle of the night, God visited, healed, and delivered you. You get to tell the story but "Who" gets the glory... "You Owe God Praise!"

When you could not pay your bills, you still had a roof over your head. You had food even when you did not have exactly what your taste buds wanted to eat; nourishment was provided for you to put in your belly. Your closet isn't full of the latest apparel but there are outfits hanging in there for you to put on your body. There's not a lot of money in your bank account, however you're not broke! You have money in there to count. Who supplied your every need? "You Owe God Praise!"

Your wayward child, your unsaved loved one, that close friend dealing with addiction issues, they are all still alive. None of them died in their sins. There is still time for all of them to give up on sinning and turn their life over to Him. Who kept them...? "You Owe God Praise!"

So regardless of what you are still waiting on God to do, the one important fact that will always remain is... "You Owe God Praise!"

Pray the Prayer of Faith

Heavenly Father, thank YOU for everything YOU have done for me. I'm grateful to YOU for supplying all of my need. 'YOU have never left or forsaken me.'[80] When I think of YOUR goodness and all YOU have done for me, I begin to reflect upon who I am. "...what is man, that thou art mindful of him?"[81] I will continue to praise YOU for the things YOU have done, for the things I have and even for the things I have yet to see. For surely, I know YOU will bring my desires to pass. I will continue to honor YOU. I will continue to worship YOU. I will continue to love, serve, and trust YOU for the rest of my days. YOUR "...praise shall continually be in my mouth."[82] In Jesus' name I pray. Amen.

CHAPTER FOURTEEN

Secret Confession

"...yea, I have spoken it, I will also bring it to pass, I have purposed it, I will do it."[83]

Have you ever been holding onto something confidential that you've been confessing privately? You've held onto it for so long you felt as if you were going to burst with excitement if you did not get it out? You were contemplating waiting for what you saw in your spirit to happen in the natural before you released it.

However, you could not keep it to yourself, and you had to share it with someone. With what you thought to be careful consideration, you unleashed what was leaping on the inside of you to someone you thought would celebrate with you; only to find out after revealing it to the individual that this person was part of the hater's club. You thought that he/she would be happy for you because this person wasn't someone you just met. The two of you had been walking closely together for some time. You assumed this individual would rejoice with you.

You did not expect him/her to react like he/she did. You shared in the manifested joys of their visions and dreams. You even contributed to the success of it because you called him/her a friend.

Yet to your surprise after releasing your vision to someone you thought would be there to cheer you on, another "person" emerged.

You were taken aback when the words released out of his/her mouth were "oh that's going to be impossible for you to do."

Immediately you felt the sting and your spirit cried "JESUS what just happened!!!" Holding your composure, you thought to yourself "my God who in the world is this?!" It was at that moment that you saw through those words and directly into his/her heart.

DON'T SANCTION ANYTHING THAT MAY TRY TO HINDER OR TERMINATE WHAT GOD HAS PREDETERMINED FOR YOU TO DO.

The person's facial expression and body language displayed everything you were feeling, hearing and even the things that weren't verbally voiced.

Your mind recalled occasions when you were excited and rejoiced when God blessed him/her before and after it came to pass. However, the one thing that remained true was he/she wasn't the least bit happy for you.

Before sharing your vision, you already knew it would be impossible for you to do because the mental images you were envisioning were so much bigger than you. You knew it would take all of God, His resources and His divine connections that you hadn't yet possessed. Nevertheless. you kept the vision before you. Although you did not have a clue as to how the resources and connections you needed were going to make its way to you, you tucked it away in your spirit and rested in the fact that if God gave you the vision that it would be His responsibility to bring it to pass.

With an already made-up mind, you did not let those words ruin it for you. You dismissed every word out of your head because you knew what spirit was behind it. You didn't even try to make sense out of what had just happened. When the red flag went up, your spirit alerted you that it was time to move on because this was one of those undesirable relationships.

Beloved, if you haven't been faced with this situation, one day you will. It's called the weeding process. Everybody won't be able to handle what God is going to do through you and where He will take you. During the weeding season, three things will occur with people in your life. Some are meant to be there for a lifetime, others only stay for a season, and then there are those who only stop by for a reason. Count it all joy. Everybody cannot go along for the ride.

In the meantime, SHUT—OUT all negativity and distractions to whatever is trying to oppose the visions and dreams that God has placed in your spirit to do. Treat all negativity and distractions as wood, hay, and stubble, because negativity and distractions have their place in the lake of fire, too.

Remember, God has the final say and God will NEVER change His mind. "For verily I say unto you, Till heaven and earth pass, one jot or one tittle shall in no wise pass from the law, till all be fulfilled."[84] Lastly, I'm going to throw this in here for free because I write to encourage you. Never allow the mindset of another to cause you to abort your visions and dreams.

Hold on, keep the faith, nurture, and cultivate God's seed and believe that God will bring it to pass in your lifetime. If God said it, God will make good on His promise if you continue to stand firm in whom and what you believe.

Keep God's vision alive in your spirit at all costs. Don't sanction anything that may try to hinder or terminate what God has predetermined for you to do. Opposition always produces an opportunity for God to be glorified!

As sad as it may be, and as quiet as it may be kept, everybody will not be happy for you. For whatever reason, people choose to be unenthusiastic, unsupportive and show signs of opposition, don't allow their thoughts to cloud the visions and dreams God has given you! Let that experience serve as a reminder. Be careful who you share your visions and dreams with. Before sharing what is in your spirit with anyone, before you release anything, make sure it's God who is telling you to reveal it, and not you (or the excitement of what God is going to do).

Pray the Prayer of Faith

God, I thank YOU for being God in my life and for entrusting me to do great and mighty exploits for YOU, Lord. Although the vision I see is so much larger than me, I know with YOUR MIGHTY HAND it will all come to pass. Thank YOU, God, for giving me visions and dreams so great that only YOU will be able to receive the glory. I turn a deaf ear to every naysayer, hater, and negative word. I will keep my eyes on YOU, Lord. Every form of opposition will have no other choice but to acknowledge that "...This is the Lord's doing; it is marvelous in our eyes."[85] YOU shall get the glory, honor, and praise out of every manifested vision and dream. I love YOU, Lord. It is in Jesus' name I pray this prayer, Amen.

CHAPTER FIFTEEN

Shake The Dust

We are living in a culture where people are doing and saying whatever they deem necessary in order to excel in life.

Nowadays, it does not matter what a person has to do or say to get where he/she wants to go. Nor does it matter what a person has to do or say to get what he/she desires to have. These individuals will use extreme measures and sometimes will flat out lie. They will even devise a scheme in order to destroy a person's integrity by assassinating their character with the very intent to bring on their demise.

What would make a person go so far as to try to ruin another person's reputation by making malicious, untrue, and slanderous accusations against them?

Whatever the reason, he/she sees you as a threat and makes up in his/her mind that it wouldn't be good for you to stay around. So, they use unimaginable methods by going out of their way to paint a picture of incompetency, and at the same time, they label you a troublemaker.

It's quite disturbing to see all the effort and energy that is put into making someone else look bad. It's just useless exertion on their part and it's simply appalling. All that wasted time and drive could have been used on being positive and productive. Instead, the time was utilized by wreaking havoc in an attempt to cause destruction in the lives of others. This is utterly alarming. The sad thing about this is the person carrying out these evil deeds takes pleasure in what they have done.

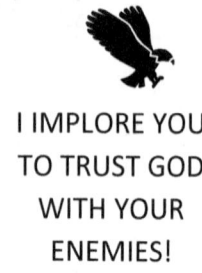

I IMPLORE YOU TO TRUST GOD WITH YOUR ENEMIES!

Rule of Thumb: 'Never sow seeds for a harvest you don't want to reap.'[86] Tainting someone else's reputation will always result in a reaped "unwanted" harvest for the initiator. "Recompense to no man evil for evil..."[87]

I implore you to trust God with your enemies! This battle is not yours. I'm a living testament that if you keep your hands clean and a pure heart, God will vindicate you in due season. Remember the fight is not about you; it's about what God is doing in and through you. Stay focused. The fight is fixed. You already win.

I encourage you to continue in pursuit of your kingdom responsibilities! Stay committed to doing unto others as you would have them do unto you.

"When a man's ways please the Lord, he maketh even his enemies to be at peace with him."[88]

Pray the Prayer of Faith

Father, in Jesus' name, I thank YOU for ruling and reigning in my life. YOU are there even in the midst of accusers that rise up against me planning and plotting evil to discredit me by scandalizing my name in attempt to humiliate me by assassinating my character. God YOUR WORD conveys that, "...A good name is rather to be chosen"[89] I'm so glad that I bear YOUR NAME. YOU see all and YOU hear all and YOU know all. I put my trust in YOU, God. I know at the right time, YOU will vindicate me. Thank YOU, God, for 'delivering me out of the hands of my enemies.'[90] In Jesus' Name I pray, Amen.

CHAPTER SIXTEEN

My People shall NEVER be put to SHAME!

Remember those earlier days after you received the light, when you endured a great conflict full of suffering? Sometimes, you were publicly exposed to insult; at other times, you stood side by side with those who were mistreated. You suffered along with those in prison and joyfully accepted the confiscation of your property, because you knew that you had better and lasting possessions.

So do not throw away your confidence; it will be richly rewarded. You need to persevere so that when you have done the Will of God, you will receive what He has promised. This is what the writer in Hebrews 10:37-39 records: "For yet a little while, and he that shall come will come, and will not tarry. Now the just shall live by faith: but if any man draw back, my soul shall have no pleasure in him. But we are not of them who draw back unto perdition; but of them that believe to the saving of the soul."[91]

Let these scriptures serve as a reminder of the encouraging promise given to you from God.

If you're like me after coming to Christ, you underwent a series of trials and tribulations that really tested your faith. There were many times when you suffered at the hands of others because of their insecurities and/or misconceptions. Even though you were mistreated, ridiculed, and made to be a public spectacle, you were there for many; standing with them, assisting them as they worked through the pains they were experiencing.

YOU WILL RECEIVE WHAT HE HAS PROMISED!

You did all this while cheerfully giving yourself to the Lord. Even as you faithfully served the Lord with your whole heart and in service, with your house in the middle of foreclosure, you stayed in the press, in the company of honor and dignity. When the repo man showed up at your door and pulled your vehicle from out of your garage, not because you chose not to pay the note but because you just did not have the money to make the payment; with consistency, you still placed your tithe and offering in the kingdom. Even in the midst of your personal belongings being taken you knew there was one thing that no one could ever take from you ... and that was JESUS the CHRIST.

Now GOD says to you….

Because you never denied MY NAME, you were able to withstand all of life's experiences and encounters.
When you elected to indulge in worldly pleasures, and I began to convict and chastise you, you acknowledged ME. You repented and turned from sin and began to serve ME with your heart, spirit, mind, soul, and body. When the enemy noticed you were no longer his, I allowed him to repeatedly hurl "…fiery darts…"[92] at you but even in his attempt to win you, you didn't give in. You could have run in the opposite direction; instead, you kept reaching for ME. When hell broke loose, making its way into every area of your life, you could have chosen to throw in the towel. However, you decided to "…take up your cross and follow me…"[93] Bailing out was never an option for you. The times when you were up and down throughout the night because there was so much on your mind and you were unable to sleep, I was with you—holding your mind together with both MY hands. When your body was aching with pain, I was there massaging your heart making it easy for you to catch your next breath. MY son, MY daughter, you hung in there and weathered every storm that violently swept through your life. When people talked about you and lied on you for no reason at all, you still looked to ME. In some of the darkest hours of your life, you, in some of the most devastating moments in your life, managed to keep your attitude and spirit right. You were not like those who turned away from ME because they were worried. On the other hand, when trying times came upon you, you ran directly to ME and

embraced ME. You called upon MY NAME and with MY guidance and instruction you conquered test after test, trial after trial, tribulation after tribulation. You had the faith that I would save you. You've been tried and proven. You've remained "...steadfast, unmovable..."[94] Through every tear, 'you continued to plow and harvest MY field.'[95] You stood only for MY cause even when you stood alone. I know I can trust you. You're a warrior. You are a champion! I AM proud of you. YOU are MY Child. Your faithfulness has brought you to a new day. Your labor of love has been noted. I have favored you. Your reward is due. Now I WILL compensate you. Continue to AIM HIGH.

CHAPTER SEVENTEEN

JESUS is calling YOU

A Message to the unsaved, to the backslider, to the one who has lost all hope:

God is calling YOU...
Today, it is in my spirit to tell all who will hear and obey that... If you're not in right Standing with GOD, there's urgency in my soul and it's crying out to you and for you. Inwardly you know who you are because the Spirit of God is speaking to you in this moment.

It is time to completely SURRENDER, be SAVED and SUBMIT your life to God in every way, in every area, every day. God is the only ONE who can make a reservation for you in HEAVEN or HELL.

I have made my choice and I would love to see all of you in heaven the day God cracks open the sky. My destination to Heaven is cleared. My reservation has been made; now my job is to help bring in lost souls.

Therefore, this is in no way a goodbye. I still have much work to do for God's Kingdom here in the earth. This is why I write to you today with such urgency in my heart.

For the Spirit of the Lord says this day...

"...Today if ye will hear HIS voice, harden not your hearts, as in the provocation."[96] Do not rebel against me and 'I will come in and make my abode in you'[97] and "...ye shall be free indeed."[98]

It matters what you do, it matters what you say, it matters how you live your life. It all matters to ME. It is MY desire that you be saved and spend life with ME in eternity. It does not matter what you have done in the past. I will forgive you. I love you all. No one comes to ME except by way of JESUS. I AM calling you. Will you COME?

Pray the Prayer of Salvation

Heavenly Father, I come to YOU in the name of Jesus. I acknowledge that I am a sinner. I'm in need of a Savior. I renounce all of my sins. Come into my heart Lord, Jesus and save me. I surrender my life to you. I submit my spirit, body, mind, and soul to YOU. Purify my heart, King Jesus. Hear my cry oh Lord, "...wash me..."[99] and make me whole. I want to be used by YOU. Have YOUR way. Live big in me and through me, Jesus, for the rest of my days. In Jesus' name, I count it done. Amen.

ABOUT THE AUTHOR

Kim Holmes is a native of New York. She resides in Raleigh, North Carolina with her husband Frank who has been her best friend for 48 years. Born to lead by making a difference Kim's AIM is to push and propel the people of God into their earthly assignment in spite of the trials and tribulations they have experienced and or encountered on the way to destiny.

In 2007 Kim established "3" Hours With The Father Intercessory Prayer in her home. After fervently laboring in prayer IMPACT Global Ministries (IGM) was birthed.
During one of the 6am intercessory prayer meetings the words God's Woman Man's Helpmeet was conceived within her spirit. Kim carried the dreams behind those weighty words knowing that one day these words would accomplish the purpose for which God placed them there. And as a result of it, God's Woman Man's Helpmeet (GWMH) a monthly Newsletter Publication was produced making its way into the hands of people near

and far touching lives via internet, USPS and during Church events. Praise reports poured in monthly as prayer requests sent in were answered and for that God gets the glory.

In 2011 her spirit gave way to AIM and A Inspiring Moment Blog was created to encourage the hearts of others at just the click of a finger.

Kim is a firm believer in speaking life into what looks like a dead situation in order that defeat may remain under her feet as she lifts up the name of Jesus. Her life testifies to the truth that 'with God nothing shall be impossible.'[100] because "I AM"[101] says that, "If ye abide in me, and my words abide in you, ye shall ask what ye will, and it shall be done unto you."[102]

In the midst of the pandemic in January of 2021 she founded Sisters Sharpening Sisters. SSS is an online faith community backed by Proverbs 27:17. We gather with like-minded Sisters to receive from God, share words of encouragement, inspiration, individual experiences, remarkable testimonies, divine breakthroughs, and victories. We celebrate and pray for one another. We labor collectively as we individually seek and strive to give birth to our heavenly Father' purpose and plans for our lives, while traveling the road to destiny.

Growing up as a child Kim always had the desire to help those in need. Later in life God would intensify that same desire and usher her into Prison Ministry. God's plan for her to walk through prison doors turned into a strong passion and ignited a flame within to see both men and women live a life of freedom even behind prison walls. For 19 years Kim has been committed to making a difference serving her community and has been given the opportunity to serve in a variety of roles within and outside of prison walls.

Kim's life is mounted upon God's word. She's thoroughly convinced that as long as she abides in HIM, and HIS word abides in her that "GOD IS" in the impossible. Her daily aspiration is to IMPACT lives as she IMPARTS practical biblical principles by building up and encouraging the believer until they are able to walk in dominion and authority. That's why W.I.L.D. was initiated...Women Impacting Lives Daily; a liberating ministry for all of humanity.

By not leaning to her own understanding[103] but choosing to speak, pray and stand on God's Promised Word Kim has seen the Hand of God move mightily not only in every area of her life but also in the life of her husband, their children, and grandchildren.

Without fail God continues to provide opportunities for Kim to pour into countless numbers of people by way of ministering His word, teaching, mentoring, coaching, counseling, praying with and interceding for.

In conclusion Kim says being anything else other than the person God created an individual to be is a personal choice. It's time to stop blaming God for idiosyncrasies and become the person God intended for them to be. It's time to mount up and run with purpose. However, the key to mounting up is completely letting go.

AIM HIGH... and Soar in JESUS' Name.

Endnotes

Page 1:
[1]Jeremiah 29:11 The Holy Bible: Authorized King James Version. (1988). Nashville: Holman Bible Publishers.

Page 2:
[2]reference to 1 Corinthians 2:16 The Holy Bible: Authorized King James Version. (1988). Nashville: Holman Bible Publishers.

Page 3:
[3]Paraphrase of Matthew 14:22-26 The Holy Bible: Authorized King James Version. (1988). Nashville: Holman Bible Publishers.
[4]Matthew 14:27-29a The Holy Bible: Authorized King James Version. (1988). Nashville: Holman Bible Publishers.
[5]Paraphrase of Matthew 14:29b-30a The Holy Bible: Authorized King James Version. (1988). Nashville: Holman Bible Publishers.
[6]Paraphrase of Matthew 14:30b The Holy Bible: Authorized King James Version. (1988). Nashville: Holman Bible Publishers.

Page 3-4:
[7]Matthew 14:31-32 The Holy Bible: Authorized King James Version. (1988). Nashville: Holman Bible Publishers.

Page 4:
[8]Paraphrase of Matthew 14:29a The Holy Bible: Authorized King James Version. (1988). Nashville: Holman Bible Publishers.

Page 10:
[9]Galatians 6:1 The Holy Bible: Authorized King James Version. (1988). Nashville: Holman Bible Publishers.

[10]Paraphrase of Galatians 6:1 The Holy Bible: Authorized King James Version. (1988). Nashville: Holman Bible Publishers.

[11]Matthew 16:26 The Holy Bible: Authorized King James Version. (1988). Nashville: Holman Bible Publishers.

[12]2 Chronicles 7:14 The Holy Bible: Authorized King James Version. (1988). Nashville: Holman Bible Publishers.

[13]Isaiah 55:3 The Holy Bible: Authorized King James Version. (1988). Nashville: Holman Bible Publishers.

[14]Paraphrase of Isaiah 55:3 The Holy Bible: Authorized King James Version. (1988). Nashville: Holman Bible Publishers.

[15]Luke 4:4b The Holy Bible: Authorized King James Version. (1988). Nashville: Holman Bible Publishers.

Page 15:
[16]Paraphrase of Matthew 9:37 The Holy Bible: Authorized King James Version. (1988). Nashville: Holman Bible Publishers.

[17]Matthew 9:37 The Holy Bible: Authorized King James Version. (1988). Nashville: Holman Bible Publishers.

[18]Matthew 9:38 The Holy Bible: Authorized King James Version. (1988). Nashville: Holman Bible Publishers.

[19] Paraphrase of Matthew 9:38 The Holy Bible: Authorized King James Version. (1988). Nashville: Holman Bible Publishers.

[20] Paraphrase of Ephesians 4:11 The Holy Bible: Authorized King James Version. (1988). Nashville: Holman Bible Publishers.

Page 16:

[21] Matthew 9:35-38 The Holy Bible: Authorized King James Version. (1988). Nashville: Holman Bible Publishers.

[22] Paraphrase of Acts 1:8 The Holy Bible: Authorized King James Version. (1988). Nashville: Holman Bible Publishers.

[23] Acts 1:8 The Holy Bible: Authorized King James Version. (1988). Nashville: Holman Bible Publishers.

[24] Matthew 9:38 The Holy Bible: Authorized King James Version. (1988). Nashville: Holman Bible Publishers.

[25] Paraphrase of Matthew 9:35-38 The Holy Bible: Authorized King James Version. (1988). Nashville: Holman Bible Publishers.

Page 21:

[26] John 3:16 The Holy Bible: Authorized King James Version. (1988). Nashville: Holman Bible Publishers.

[27] Psalm 8: 4-6 The Holy Bible: Authorized King James Version. (1988). Nashville: Holman Bible Publishers.

Page 22:

[28] 2 Corinthians 5:21 The Holy Bible: Authorized King James Version. (1988). Nashville: Holman Bible Publishers.

[29] 1 Samuel 15:22 The Holy Bible: Authorized King James Version. (1988). Nashville: Holman Bible Publishers.

[30]Matthew16:24 The Holy Bible: Authorized King James Version. (1988). Nashville: Holman Bible Publishers.

Page 27:
[31]Acts 16:25 The Holy Bible: Authorized King James Version. (1988). Nashville: Holman Bible Publishers.

[32]Paraphrase of Acts 16:22-25 The Holy Bible: Authorized King James Version. (1988). Nashville: Holman Bible Publishers

[33]Paraphrae of Acts 16:25 The Holy Bible: Authorized King James Version. (1988). Nashville: Holman Bible Publishers.

Page 28:
[34]Paraphrase of Acts 16:25 The Holy Bible: Authorized King James Version. (1988). Nashville: Holman Bible Publishers.

[35]Proverbs 18:24 The Holy Bible: Authorized King James Version. (1988). Nashville: Holman Bible Publishers.

Page 33:
[36]Paraphrase of Matthew 18:21-23 The Holy Bible: Authorized King James Version. (1988). Nashville: Holman Bible Publishers.

[37]Matthew 18:21-23 The Holy Bible: Authorized King James Version. (1988). Nashville: Holman Bible Publishers.

Page 34:
[38]Paraphrase of Matthew 18:23 The Holy Bible: Authorized King James Version. (1988). Nashville: Holman Bible Publishers.

Page 34-35:

[39] Matthew 18:23-34 The Holy Bible: Authorized King James Version. (1988). Nashville: Holman Bible Publishers.

Page 35:
[40] Philippians 4:13 The Holy Bible: Authorized King James Version. (1988). Nashville: Holman Bible Publishers.
[41] Paraphrase of Ephesians 4:32 The Holy Bible: Authorized King James Version. (1988). Nashville: Holman Bible Publishers.

Page 40:
[42] Paraphrase of 2 Peter 1 The Holy Bible: Authorized King James Version. (1988). Nashville: Holman Bible Publishers.
[43] Psalm 37:23a The Holy Bible: Authorized King James Version. (1988). Nashville: Holman Bible Publishers.
[44] Jeremiah 29:11 The Holy Bible: Authorized King James Version. (1988). Nashville: Holman Bible Publishers.

Page 41:
[45] Paraphrase of 2 Peter 1:3 The Holy Bible: Authorized King James Version. (1988). Nashville: Holman Bible Publishers.

Page 46:
[46] Jeremiah 8:22 The Holy Bible: Authorized King James Version. (1988). Nashville: Holman Bible Publishers.

Page 46-47:
[47] 1 Thessalonians 5:18 The Holy Bible: Authorized King James Version. (1988). Nashville: Holman Bible Publishers.

Page 47:
[48] Hebrews 12: 2a The Holy Bible: Authorized King James Version. (1988). Nashville: Holman Bible Publishers.

[49] Psalm 139:8 The Holy Bible: Authorized King James Version. (1988). Nashville: Holman Bible Publishers.

[50] Paraphrase of Jeremiah 8:22 The Holy Bible: Authorized King James Version. (1988). Nashville: Holman Bible Publishers.

Page 51:

[51] Haggai 1:5 The Holy Bible: Authorized King James Version. (1988). Nashville: Holman Bible Publishers.

Page 52:

[52] Galatians 6:7 The Holy Bible: Authorized King James Version. (1988). Nashville: Holman Bible Publishers.

[53] Ephesians 5:13 The Holy Bible: Authorized King James Version. (1988). Nashville: Holman Bible Publishers.

[54] Paraphrase of John 4: 24 The Holy Bible: Authorized King James Version. (1988). Nashville: Holman Bible Publishers.

[55] Matthew 6:24 The Holy Bible: Authorized King James Version. (1988). Nashville: Holman Bible Publishers.

[56] Paraphrase of Exodus 20:16 The Holy Bible: Authorized King James Version. (1988). Nashville: Holman Bible Publishers.

[57] 1 Peter 1:16 The Holy Bible: Authorized King James Version. (1988). Nashville: Holman Bible Publishers.

[58] Haggai 1:5 The Holy Bible: Authorized King James Version. (1988). Nashville: Holman Bible Publishers.

[59] 2 Corinthians 5:15-17 The Holy Bible: Authorized King James Version. (1988). Nashville: Holman Bible Publishers.

Page 57:

[60] Proverbs 18:21 The Holy Bible: Authorized King James Version. (1988). Nashville: Holman Bible Publishers.

Page 58:
[61]James 3:5-10 The Holy Bible: Authorized King James Version. (1988). Nashville: Holman Bible Publishers.

Page 63:
[62]Paraphrase of Hebrews 12:1 The Holy Bible: Authorized King James Version. (1988). Nashville: Holman Bible Publishers.

[63]James 1:4 The Holy Bible: Authorized King James Version. (1988). Nashville: Holman Bible Publishers.

[64]Numbers 23:19 The Holy Bible: Authorized King James Version. (1988). Nashville: Holman Bible Publishers.

[65]Paraphrase of Isaiah 55:11 The Holy Bible: Authorized King James Version. (1988). Nashville: Holman Bible Publishers.

[66]Paraphrase of James 1:6 The Holy Bible: Authorized King James Version. (1988). Nashville: Holman Bible Publishers.

Page 64:
[67]James 1:2-8,12 The Holy Bible: Authorized King James Version. (1988). Nashville: Holman Bible Publishers.

[68]Hebrews 12:1 The Holy Bible: Authorized King James Version. (1988). Nashville: Holman Bible Publishers.

page 69:
[69]Paraphrase of 1 Samuel 13:14 The Holy Bible: Authorized King James Version. (1988). Nashville: Holman Bible Publishers.

Page 69-70:
[70]Paraphrase of 2 Samuel 12 The Holy Bible: Authorized King James Version. (1988). Nashville: Holman Bible Publishers.

Page 70:
[71]Proverbs 3: 6-12 The Holy Bible: Authorized King James Version. (1988). Nashville: Holman Bible Publishers.

Page 71:
[72]Paraphrase of Proverbs 4:20-22 The Holy Bible: Authorized King James Version. (1988). Nashville: Holman Bible Publishers.

[73]Proverbs 4:20-25 The Holy Bible: Authorized King James Version. (1988). Nashville: Holman Bible Publishers.

Page 71-72:
[74]Proverbs 4:20-27 The Holy Bible: Authorized King James Version. (1988). Nashville: Holman Bible Publishers.

Page 72:
[75]Paraphrase of Hebrews 8:12 The Holy Bible: Authorized King James Version. (1988). Nashville: Holman Bible Publishers.

[76]Psalm 71:8 The Holy Bible: Authorized King James Version. (1988). Nashville: Holman Bible Publishers.

[77]Jeremiah 29:11 The Holy Bible: Authorized King James Version. (1988). Nashville: Holman Bible Publishers.

[78]Galatians 5:22-23 The Holy Bible: Authorized King James Version. (1988). Nashville: Holman Bible Publishers.

Page 77:
[79]Paraphrase of Psalm 23:6 The Holy Bible: Authorized King James Version. (1988). Nashville: Holman Bible Publishers.

Page 78-79:
[80]Paraphrase of Hebrews 13:5c The Holy Bible: Authorized King James Version. (1988). Nashville: Holman Bible Publishers.

Page 79:
[81]Psalm 8:4 The Holy Bible: Authorized King James Version. (1988). Nashville: Holman Bible Publishers.

[82]Paraphrase of Psalm 34: 1c The Holy Bible: Authorized King James Version. (1988). Nashville: Holman Bible Publishers.

Page 83:
[83]Isaiah 46:11 The Holy Bible: Authorized King James Version. (1988). Nashville: Holman Bible Publishers.

Page 85:
[84]Matthew 5:18 The Holy Bible: Authorized King James Version. (1988). Nashville: Holman Bible Publishers.

Page 85-86:
[85]Psalm 118:23 The Holy Bible: Authorized King James Version. (1988). Nashville: Holman Bible Publishers.

Page 91-92:
[86]Paraphrase of Galatians 6:7 The Holy Bible: Authorized King James Version. (1988). Nashville: Holman Bible Publishers.

Page 92:
[87]Romans 12:17a The Holy Bible: Authorized King James Version. (1988). Nashville: Holman Bible Publishers.

[88]Proverbs 16:7 The Holy Bible: Authorized King James Version. (1988). Nashville: Holman Bible Publishers.

[89]Proverbs 22:1a The Holy Bible: Authorized King James Version. (1988). Nashville: Holman Bible Publishers.

[90]Paraphrase of Psalms 31:15b The Holy Bible: Authorized King James Version. (1988). Nashville: Holman Bible Publishers.

Page 97:
[91]Hebrews 10:37-39 The Holy Bible: Authorized King James Version. (1988). Nashville: Holman Bible Publishers.

Page 98:
[92]Ephesians 6:16 The Holy Bible: Authorized King James Version. (1988). Nashville: Holman Bible Publishers.

[93]Matthew 16:24-26 The Holy Bible: Authorized King James Version. (1988). Nashville: Holman Bible Publishers.

Page 99:
[94]1 Corinthians 15:58 The Holy Bible: Authorized King James Version. (1988). Nashville: Holman Bible Publishers.

[95]Paraphrase of Luke 10:2 The Holy Bible: Authorized King James Version. (1988). Nashville: Holman Bible Publishers.

Page 103:
[96]Hebrews 3:15 The Holy Bible: Authorized King James Version. (1988). Nashville: Holman Bible Publishers.

[97]Paraphrase of John 14:23c The Holy Bible: Authorized King James Version. (1988). Nashville: Holman Bible Publishers.

[98]John 8:36 The Holy Bible: Authorized King James Version. (1988). Nashville: Holman Bible Publishers.

Page 104:
[99]Psalm 51:7 c The Holy Bible: Authorized King James Version. (1988). Nashville: Holman Bible Publishers.

Page 110:

[100]Paraphrase of Luke 1:37 The Holy Bible: Authorized King James Version. (1988). Nashville: Holman Bible Publishers.

[101]Exodus 3:14 The Holy Bible: Authorized King James Version. (1988). Nashville: Holman Bible Publishers.

[102]John 15:7 The Holy Bible: Authorized King James Version. (1988). Nashville: Holman Bible Publishers.

[103]Paraphrase of Proverbs 3:5b The Holy Bible: Authorized King James Version. (1988). Nashville: Holman Bible Publishers.

www.ingramcontent.com/pod-product-compliance
Lightning Source LLC
Chambersburg PA
CBHW071906070526
44583CB00016B/1868